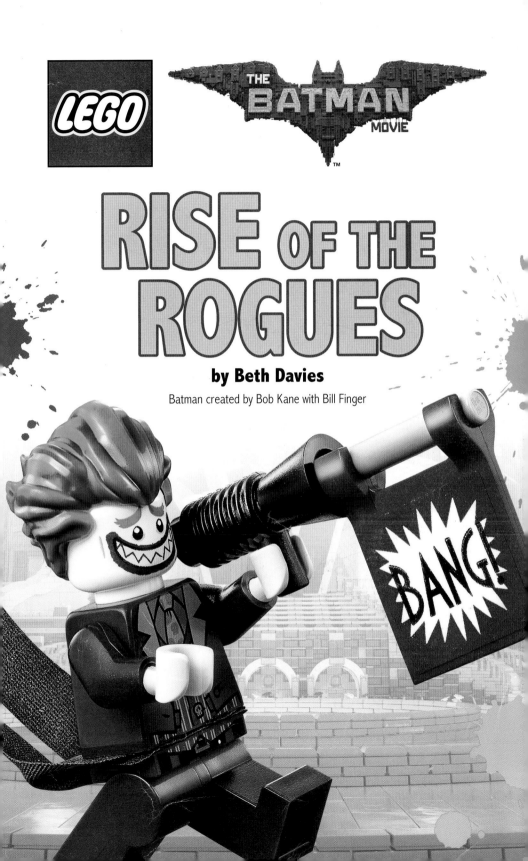

RISE OF THE ROGUES

by Beth Davies

Batman created by Bob Kane with Bill Finger

Editor Pamela Afram
Designer Sam Bartlett
Senior Editor Hannah Dolan
Senior Designer Nathan Martin
Pre-production Producer Siu Yin Chan
Producer Louise Daly
Managing Editor Paula Regan
Design Managers Guy Harvey and Jo Connor
Publisher Julie Ferris
Art Director Lisa Lanzarini
Publishing Director Simon Beecroft

Batman created by Bob Kane with Bill Finger

First American Edition, 2017
Published in the United States by DK Publishing
345 Hudson Street, New York, New York 10014

Page design copyright © 2017 Dorling Kindersley Limited
DK, a Division of Penguin Random House LLC
17 18 19 20 10 9 8 7 6 5 4 3 2 1
001–297917–Jan/2017

A catalog record for this book is available from the
Library of Congress.

ISBN 978-1-4654-5862-9 (Hardcover)
ISBN 978-1-4654-5861-2 (Paperback)

DK books are available at special discounts when purchased
in bulk for sales promotions, premiums, fund-raising, or educational use.
For details, contact: DK Publishing Special Markets, 345 Hudson Street,
New York, New York 10014
SpecialSales@dk.com

Printed and bound in the USA

A WORLD OF IDEAS:
SEE ALL THERE IS TO KNOW

www.dk.com
www.LEGO.com

Contents

Gotham City

Gotham City is a busy place, with lots of citizens.

Commissioner Jim Gordon is the Head of Police. It is his job to stop crime in the city.

Jim is soon going to retire from the job. His daughter, Barbara, is going to take over.

The Hero Team

Sometimes, Gotham City
needs heroes! When a mission
is too dangerous for the police
alone, the police commissioner
shines the Bat-Signal.
Batman sees its light shining
and rushes to the rescue.
Batman likes to work alone,
but sometimes he needs help.
Robin and Batgirl help
him to catch criminals
and save the day.
Three heroes are
better than one!

COMMISSIONER JIM GORDON

—— WANTS YOU TO HELP KEEP ——

GOTHAM CITY SAFE

Citizens of Gotham City, please alert the police if you see any of the following:

 A **cat-like** woman prowling around jewelry stores.

 A man holding a giant **question mark**. Do not approach him! Conversation may cause confusion.

 A red-haired woman surrounded by wriggling **plants**.

 A man with a huge, **toothy grin**. Do not be fooled by his friendly appearance!

GOTHAM CITY POLICE DEPARTMENT

I BELIEVE IN BATMAN

KEEPING
GOTHAM CITY
SAFE

9

Meet the Rogues

Gotham City's villains have started working together, too. Their team is known as the Rogues.

Each of these crooks has fought
Batman many times in the past.
He has beaten each one alone,
but never all of them at once!
Batman will have to use all of
his gadgets to save the day.

The Joker

The Joker is Batman's foe. He likes to cause trouble and create chaos in the city. The only thing that the Joker takes seriously is committing crime.

The Joker believes he is Batman's worst enemy. Batman does not agree. This wipes the smile off the Joker's face.

My Worst Enemy
by the Joker

Batman never laughs at my jokes,
even though they are really funny!

He always tries to stop me from
getting away from crime scenes.

He thinks he is really strong,
but I always have the last laugh!

Batman likes to take pictures
without me in them!

Harley Quinn

Harley Quinn is one
of the Joker's closest
allies. She loves his silly
pranks and nasty tricks.
Her colorful costume and
bright makeup are nearly
as eye-catching as the Joker's.

Harley used to be a doctor,
but now she causes chaos.
Batman should watch out
for her swinging bat.

The Joker's Notorious Lowrider

The car can bounce up and down

Silly golden chicken decoration

Wheels spinning at top speed

Joker

The Joker and Harley Quinn drive around
Gotham City in the Joker's Notorious
Lowrider. They create as much chaos
as they can. This wacky vehicle looks
harmless, but it is perfect for scaring people!

Music system
hides button for
missile launcher

Handles for Harley
Quinn to grip on to
while skating

A missile
launcher is
hidden inside
the trunk

Horn to make people jump

The Riddler

One of the most confusing criminals in Gotham City is the Riddler. He leaves tricky puzzles at crime scenes for Batman to solve.

If Batman follows the tire tracks of the Riddler's Riddle Racer, he might be able to stop this Rogue once and for all. Or could this be another trick?

The Penguin

This businessman is no birdbrain! The Penguin controls lots of gangs in Gotham City. This has made him very rich. He wears an expensive top hat and suit.

The Penguin attacks Batman's Batcave with an army of penguin friends. His getaway vehicle is shaped like a duck.

Mr. Freeze

This frosty villain sends a chill down Batman's spine. He wears a large, armored suit that keeps him ice-cold at all times.

Mr. Freeze is a scientist. He even
invented his own freeze gun.
He attacks the Gotham City
Energy Facility with the rest of the
Rogues. When he tells the scared
workers to "freeze," they really do!

Killer Croc

Killer Croc is one of Batman's most fearsome foes. He has a powerful tail, scaly skin, and snapping teeth—just like a real crocodile!

Killer Croc's truck is perfect
for driving through swamps.
It has large wheels and a big
headlight. Killer Croc controls
the vehicle from a section at the
back. He is so big, he cannot fit
in the driver's seat!

Catwoman

This crook is very good at breaking into buildings. Catwoman loves stealing from rich people in Gotham City. Her favorite things to steal are precious gems. This jewelry shop is a perfect target!

Catwoman makes a speedy getaway on her purple motorcycle. Luckily, Robin and Batgirl are right on her tail!

CLOSED

Poison Ivy

This Rogue likes plants much more than humans. Even her outfit is inspired by flowers. She has green-fingered gloves, and she wears leaves in her red hair.

Poison Ivy has special powers. She can control all forms of plant life. Poison Ivy wants to trap Batman in her tangling tendrils.

Clayface

Clayface is the biggest
and messiest of Batman's
foes. He is made of mud,
and can transform into
different shapes. He
creates giant mud fists for
attacking his enemies.

Clayface loves to
destroy everything around
him. Batman must watch
out for the splats of mud
he fires to stick people to
the ground.

The Joker's Plan

The Joker is very smart. He has come up with a cunning plan. He wants to destroy Gotham City Energy Facility, which supplies all the power to the city. Gotham City will be in total chaos and the Joker will take over!

THE JOKER'S FUNHOUSE

Hi, everyone. It's the Joker! I have created my very own funhouse in Gotham City. Come inside. You won't be able to stop smiling. But you MUST follow these rules...

DO:

☑ Bring rubber chickens

☑ Wear purple and green

☑ Laugh at all of my jokes

DO NOT:

 Wear black (or yellow)

 Wear long black capes and drive bat-like vehicles

 Wear black cowls with pointy ears

Gotham City's Villains

The Rogues aren't the only villains in Gotham City. There are many odd outlaws committing crimes. There are villains dressed as animals, like Zebra-Man, March Harriet, and Orca.

The Mime

March Harriet

Orca

There are even villains who base their crimes on numbers, like The Calculator. All of these villains have one thing in common—they want to help the Joker defeat Batman!

Kite Man

The Eraser

Calendar Man

The Calculator

Zebra-Man

Villains vs.
the Hero Team

The Joker and his allies attack
the Gotham City Energy Facility!
It will take great teamwork for the
Hero Team to defeat the villains.

Batman takes on Clayface and
the Riddler. Robin tackles Mr.
Freeze and Killer Croc. Batgirl
battles with the Joker and Harley
Quinn. The Hero Team must win!

Locked Up

Hurrah! Batman, Batgirl, and Robin have put an end to the Joker's plan and defeated him.

All of the Rogues have been captured. They are now locked up in Arkham Asylum. Gotham City is safe once more. Thanks, Hero Team!

Quiz

1. Who is going to take over from Jim Gordon as Head of Police?

2. What kind of hat does the Penguin wear?

3. How does the police commissioner ask Batman for help?

4. How does Poison Ivy plan to trap Batman?

5. What kind of weapon does Harley Quinn use?

6. What is Catwoman's favorite thing to steal?

7. What does the Joker want to destroy?

8. Where are the Rogues now locked up?

Answers on page 48

Glossary

allies
A group of people who work together for a purpose.

Arkham Asylum
A hospital where Gotham's worst criminals are locked away.

citizen
Someone who lives in a town or city.

crook
A person who is dishonest or a criminal.

fearsome
Very frightening.

foe
An enemy or opponent.

gang
An organized group of criminals.

scientist
A person who studies science and solves problems by doing experiments.

Guide for Parents

This book is part of an exciting four-level reading series for children, developing the habit of reading widely for both pleasure and information. These chapter books have a compelling main narrative to suit your child's reading ability. Each book is designed to develop your child's reading skills, fluency, grammar awareness, and comprehension in order to build confidence and engagement when reading.

Ready for a *Level 2* book

YOUR CHILD SHOULD

- be familiar with using beginning letter sounds and context clues to figure out unfamiliar words.
- be aware of the need for a slight pause at commas and a longer one at periods.
- alter his/her expression for questions and exclamations.

A VALUABLE AND SHARED READING EXPERIENCE

For many children, reading requires much effort, but adult participation can make this both fun and easier. So here are a few tips on how to use this book with your child.

TIP 1 Check out the contents together before your child begins:

- read the text about the book on the back cover.
- flip through the book and stop to chat about the contents page together to heighten your child's interest and expectation.
- make use of unfamiliar or difficult words on the page in a brief discussion.
- chat about the nonfiction reading features used in the book, such as headings, captions, lists, or charts.

TIP 2 Support your child as he/she reads the story pages:

- give the book to your child to read and turn the pages.
- where necessary, encourage your child to break a word into syllables, sound out each one, and then flow the syllables together. Ask him/her to reread the sentence to check the meaning.
- when there's a question mark or an exclamation mark, encourage your child to vary his/her voice as he/she reads the sentence. Demonstrate how to do this if it is helpful.

TIP 3 Chat at the end of each page:

- ask questions about the text and the meaning of the words used. These help to develop comprehension skills and awareness of the language used.

A FEW ADDITIONAL TIPS

- Always encourage your child to try reading difficult words by themselves. Praise any self-corrections, for example, "I like the way you sounded out that word and then changed the way you said it, to make sense."
- Try to read together everyday. Reading little and often is best. These books are divided into manageable chapters for one reading session. However, after 10 minutes, only keep going if your child wants to read on.
- Read other books of different types to your child just for enjoyment and information.

Series consultant, **Dr. Linda Gambrell**, Distinguished Professor of Education at Clemson University, has served as President of the National Reading Conference, the College Reading Association, and the International Reading Association.

Index

Answers to the quiz on pages 44:
1. Barbara Gordon 2. A top hat 3. With the Bat-Signal
4. With her tangling tendrils 5. A swinging bat 6. Precious gems
7. Gotham City Energy Facility 8. Arkham Asylum